CW01213352

The Dancing Light

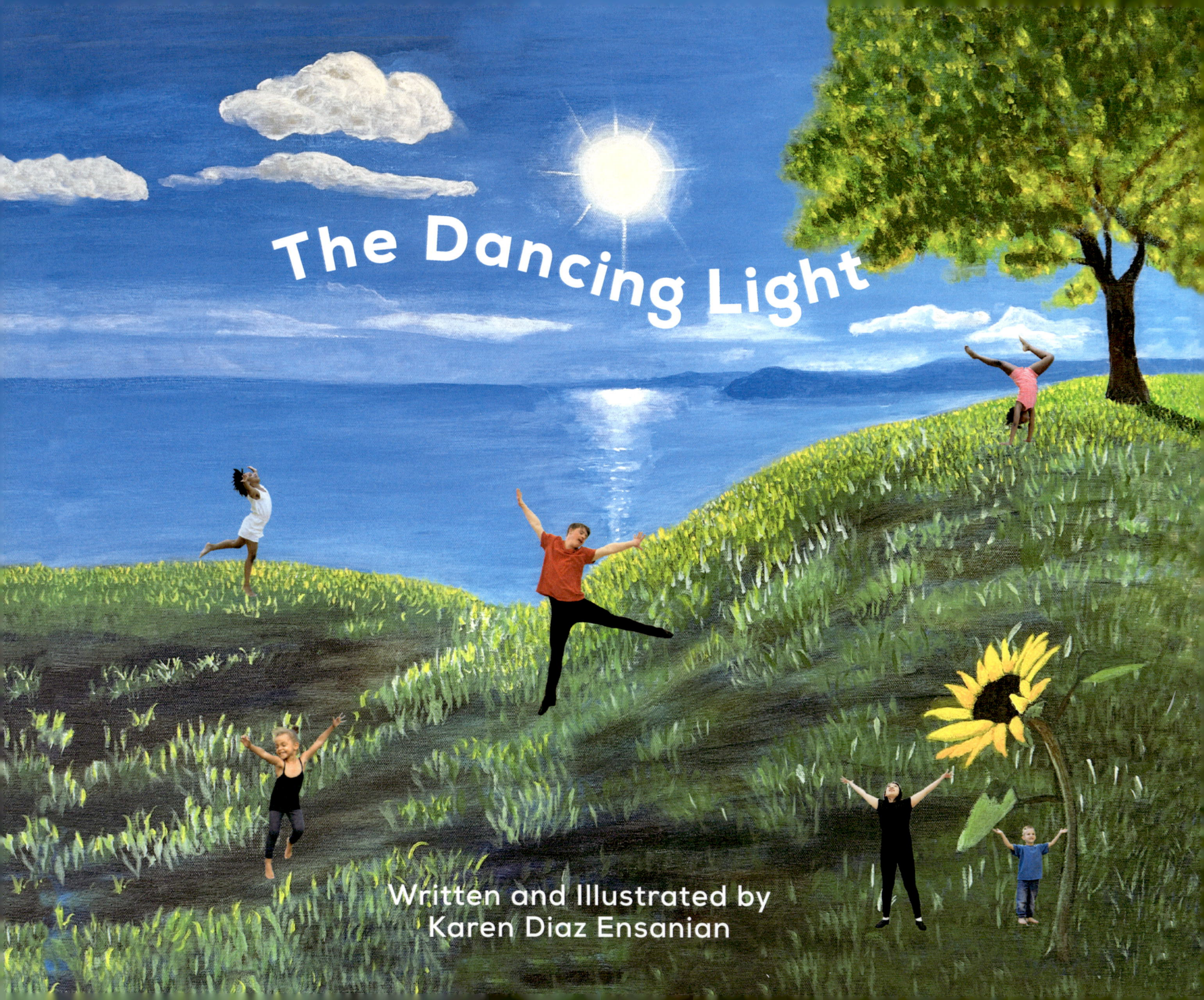

Written and Illustrated by
Karen Diaz Ensanian

Dedicated to all who love dance.

Text and Illustrations Copyright © 2022 Karen Diaz Ensanian

All rights reserved. No part of this book may be reproduced, stored in a retrieval system, or transmitted in any form or by any means, including electronic, mechanical, photocopying, recording, or otherwise without prior written permission from the publisher with exception of quoting brief passages for the purposes of review.

NOTICE
This book is intended to motivate the making of dance inspired by the nature of light. Parents, guardians, and teachers are advised to always inform children of the inherent dangers associated with electricity, water, icicles, lightning, fireworks, and any source of bright light, and to take every precaution.

ISBN: 978-0-9963919-4-8
Library of Congress Control Number: 2022904992

Published 2022 in the USA by Equus Potentia Publishing, LLC

EQUUS POTENTIA
PUBLISHING

Newton, NJ   www.equuspotentiapublishing.com

Foreword

The Dancing Light was created to help students celebrate, explore, and find connections with the nature of light through dance.

Students will develop their dance movements, guided by vocabulary, poetry, painted landscapes, and photographs of dancers in the book. With the information and imagery, the students will gain a greater understanding of light, connect this understanding in their own bodies, and internalize a deep love of the world they live in. This is an opportunity to learn through movement. At the bottom of each page there is a question that sets the dancers on a quest to find their own way of moving and creating dance.

The journey of the book follows the path of light: light found in nature, light that is man-made, the way light moves through reflection and refraction, its importance for plant life, and finally what happens when light is blocked.

Everyone can find inspiration in the dance of light.

Karen

Light is what gives our world its shapes and colors, its beauty, and its life.

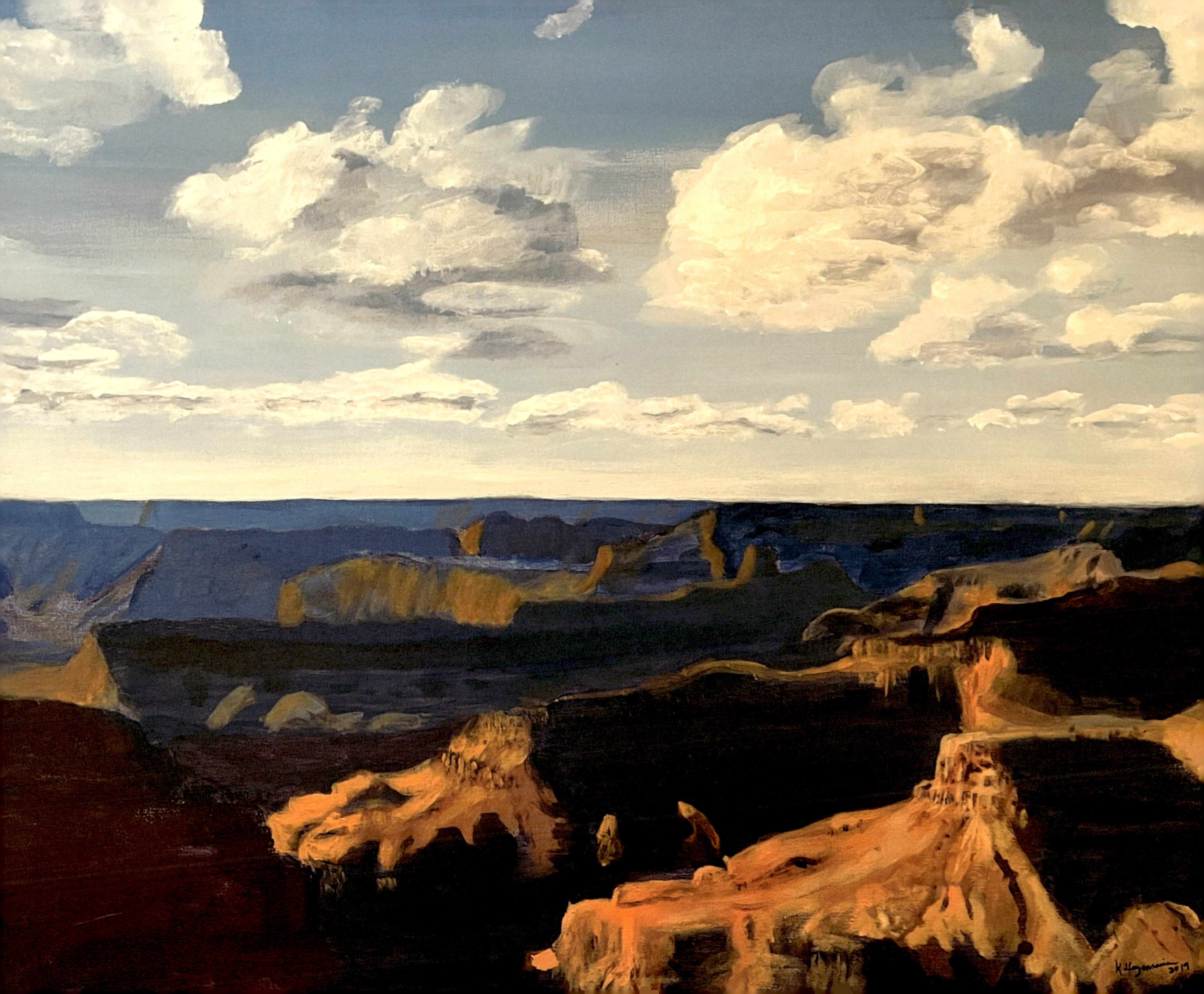
2019

As the earth rotates every day, all parts of the earth get their turn for this wonderful light.

What in nature gives us our daylight that is so bright and warm?

Sun

I shine, spread, nurture, and brighten the day.

Can you find another way to move like sunlight?

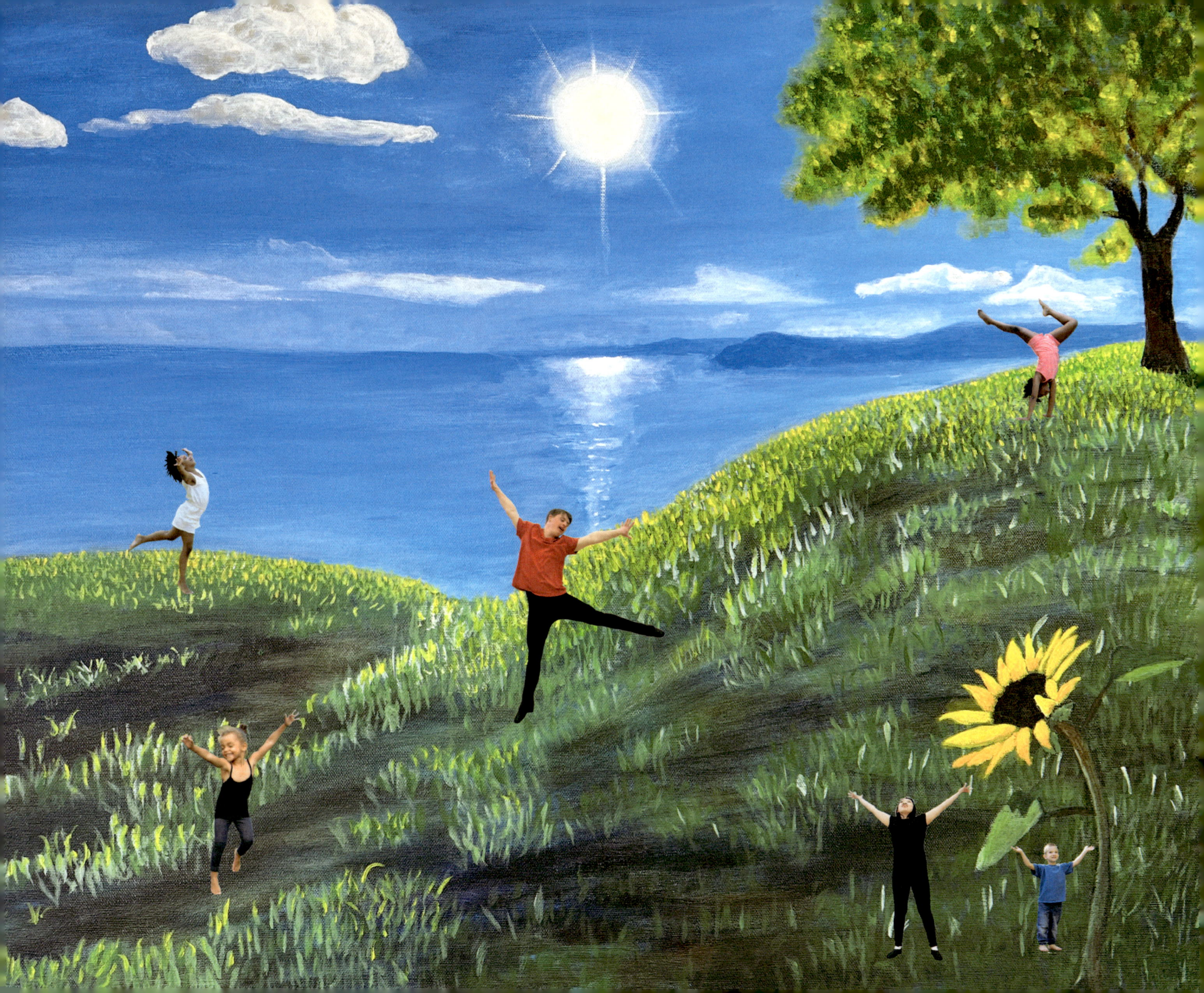

What is another kind of light found in nature?

Fire

I spark, swirl, bob, and flick. I am fire on the candle wick. Birthday, holiday, fireplace, delight. Fire, don't touch, but enjoy the warm light.

Can you find another way to move like fire?

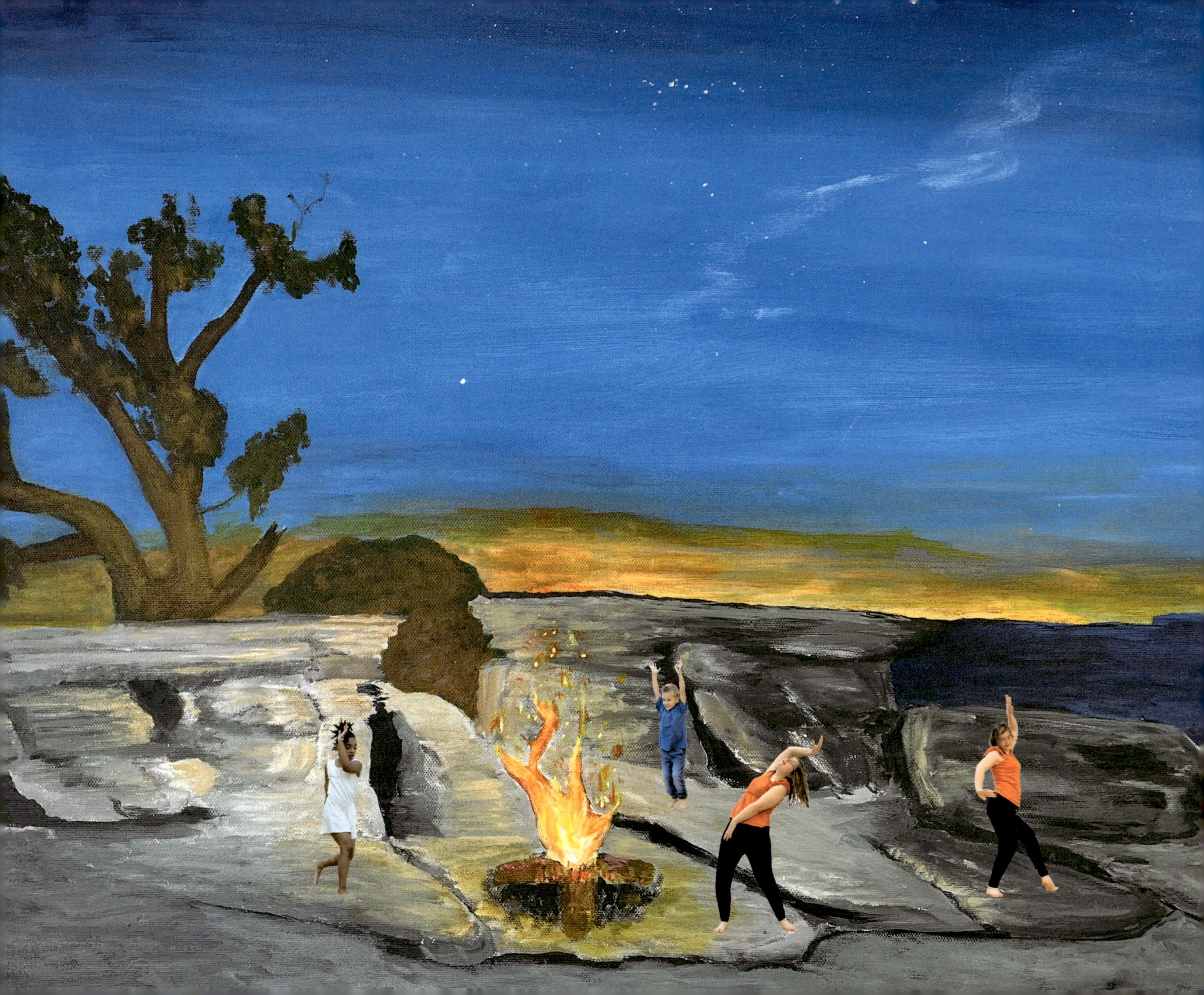

What is a creature that makes light?

Firefly

I blink, fly, hover, and rest over grasses and in trees.

Can you find another way to move like a firefly?

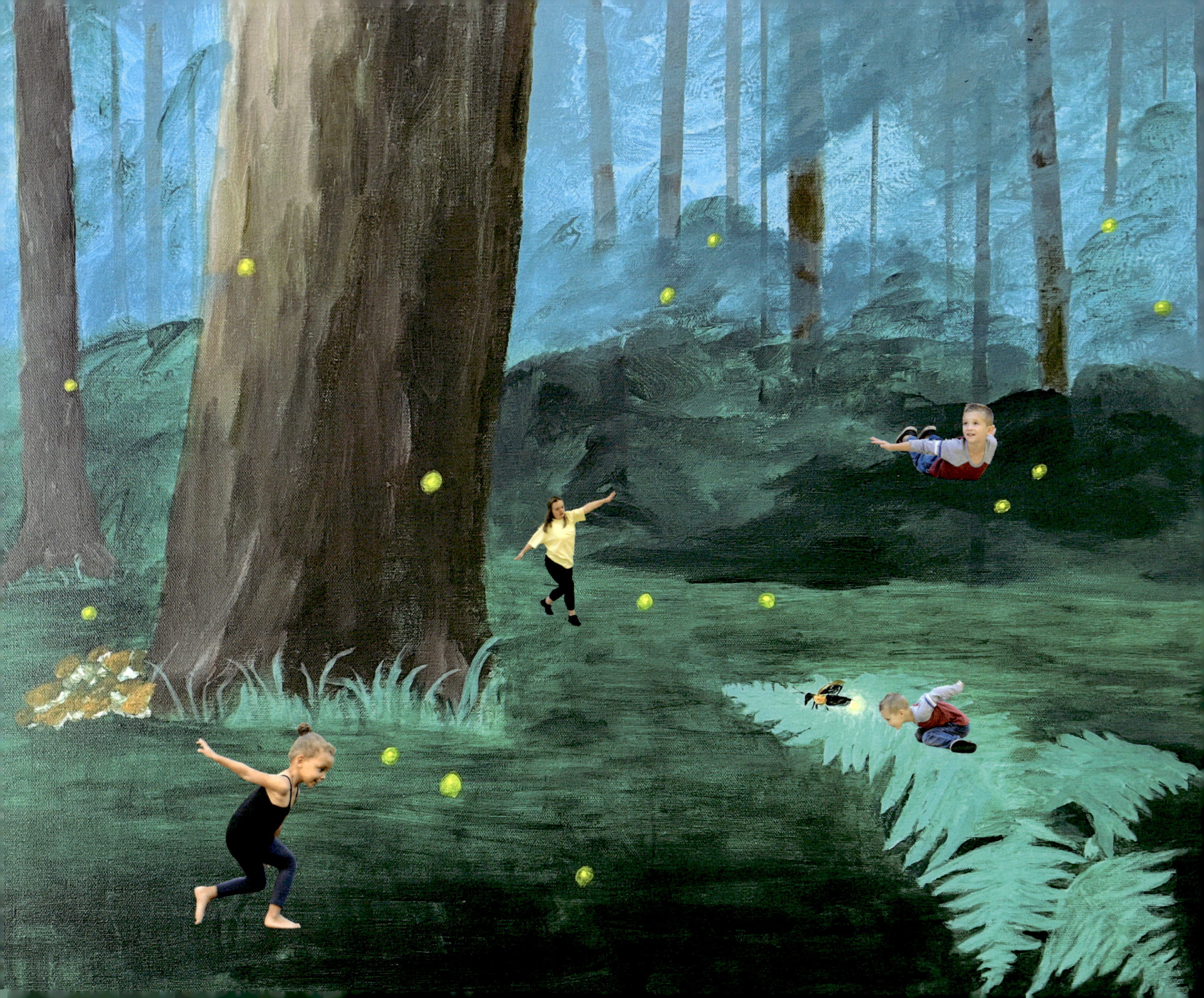

What is the light that is created in a storm cloud?

Lightning

I am electricity. I flash, streak, zigzag, crisscross, and strike.

Can you find another way to move like lightning?

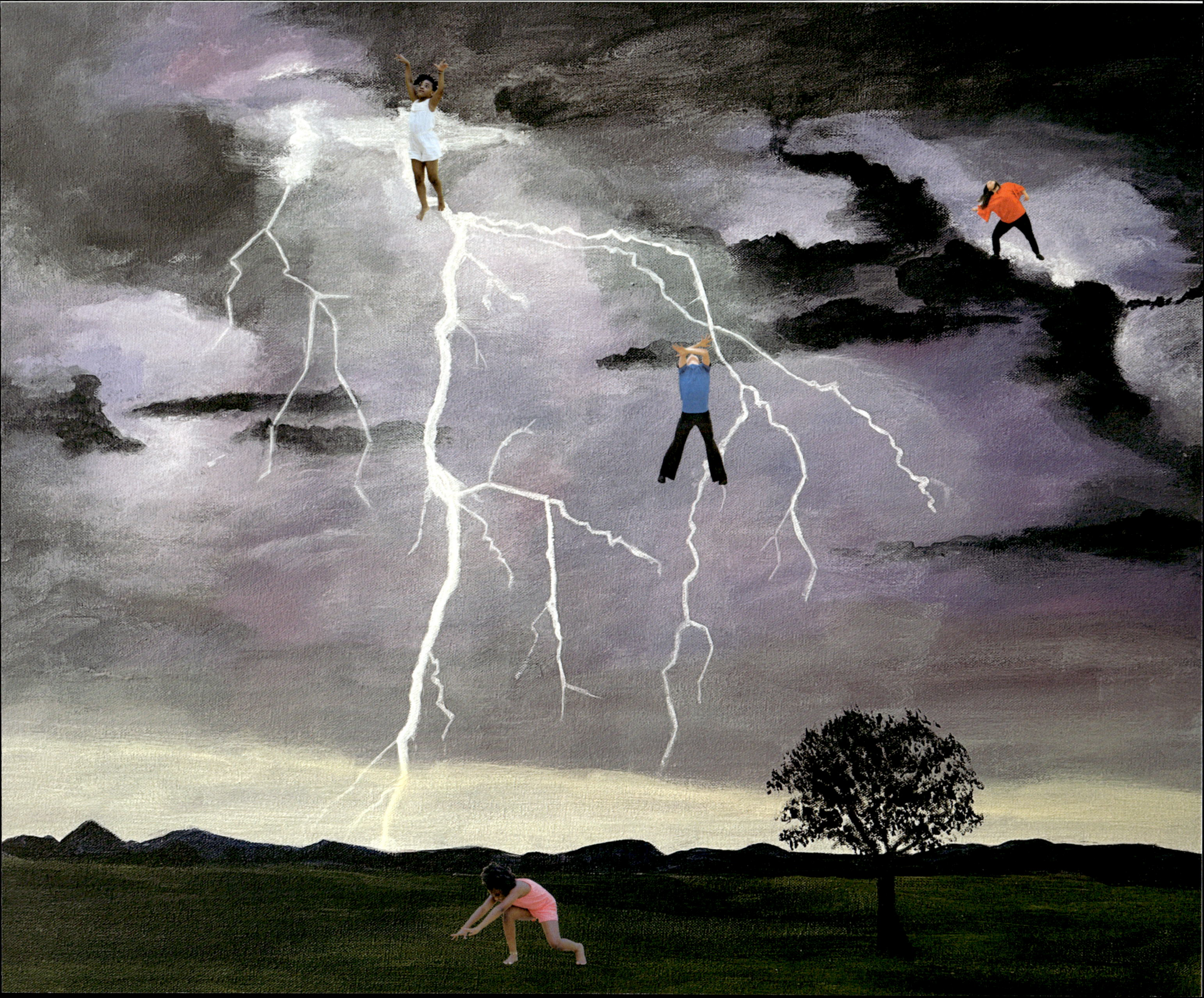

What can we use to light our buildings and streets?

Light Bulb

I am electricity racing through the thin coiling wire, twisting, burning, churning, glowing hot like fire. Lighting the path and rooms so bright, beams radiate from lamps and flashlights.

Can you find another way to move like electricity through a lightbulb?

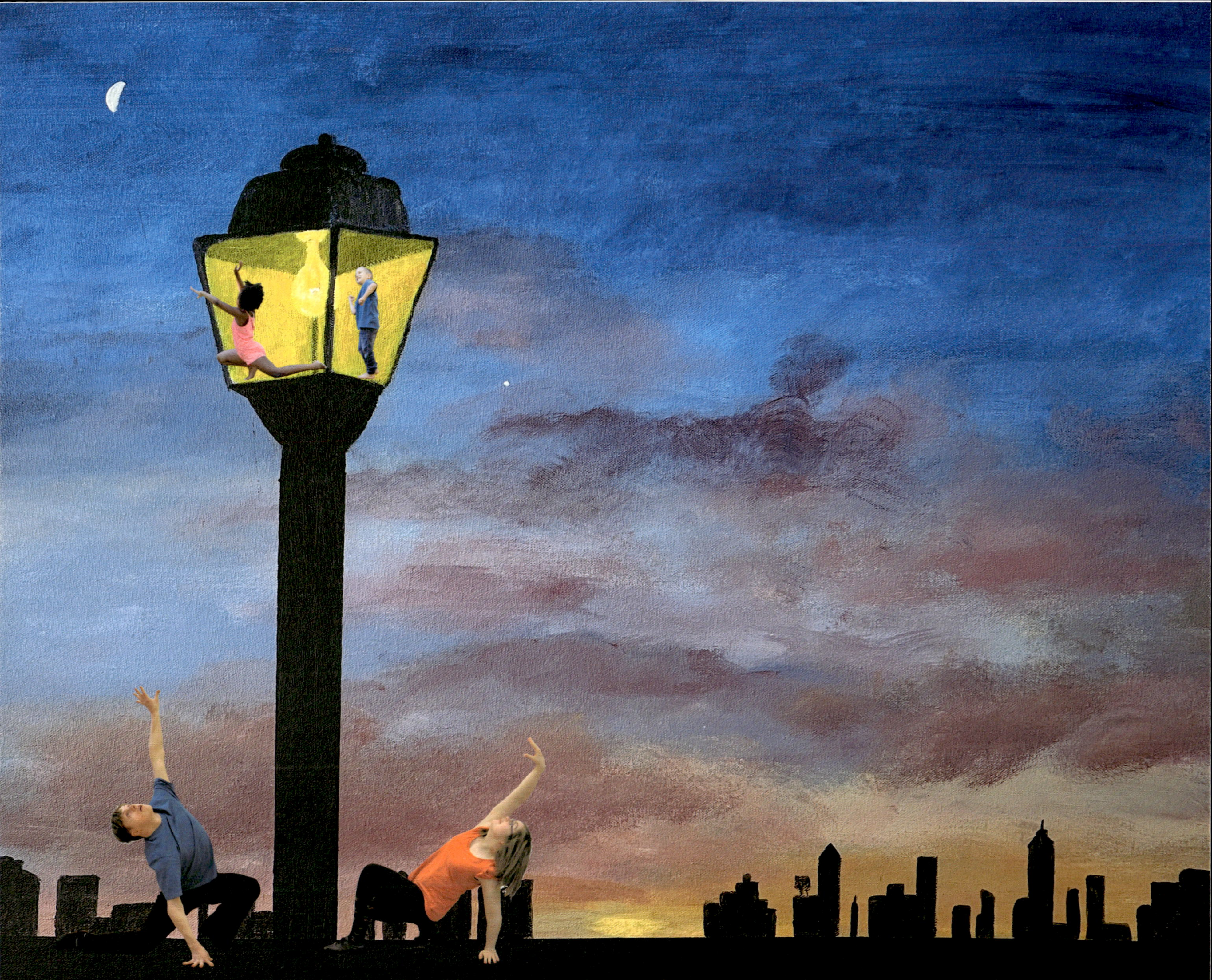

What makes light for people who want to celebrate?

Fireworks

My fuse sizzles, then I launch into the air, bursting into colors and glowing flares. Fountains of cascading light shimmer down, high in the sky spreading light all around.

Can you find another way to move like fireworks?

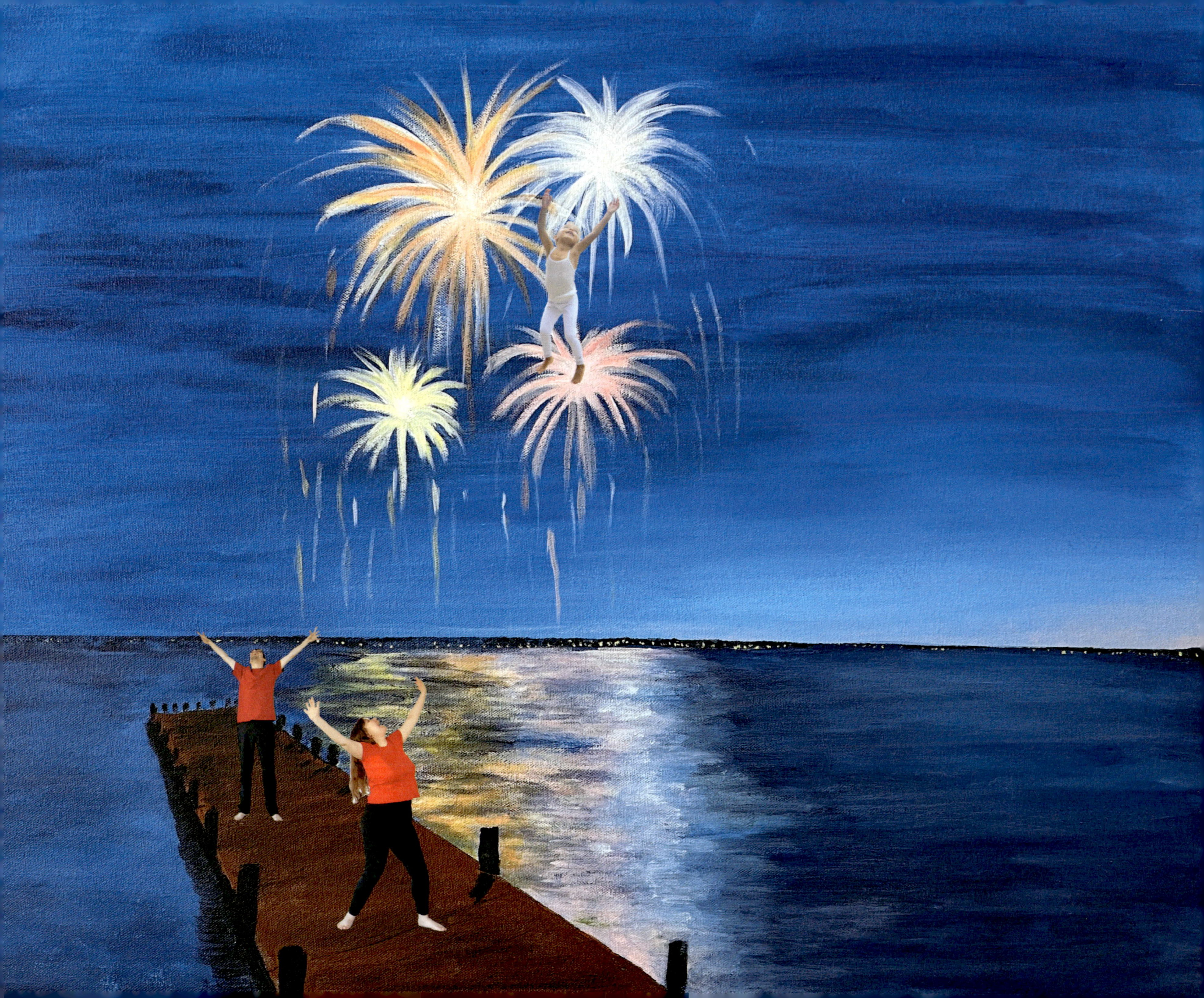

What happens to light when it hits something solid like the moon?

Reflection

I travel straight from the sun and bump into the moon. I bounce off and land on the sea and spread across the water.

Can you find another way to move like reflecting light?

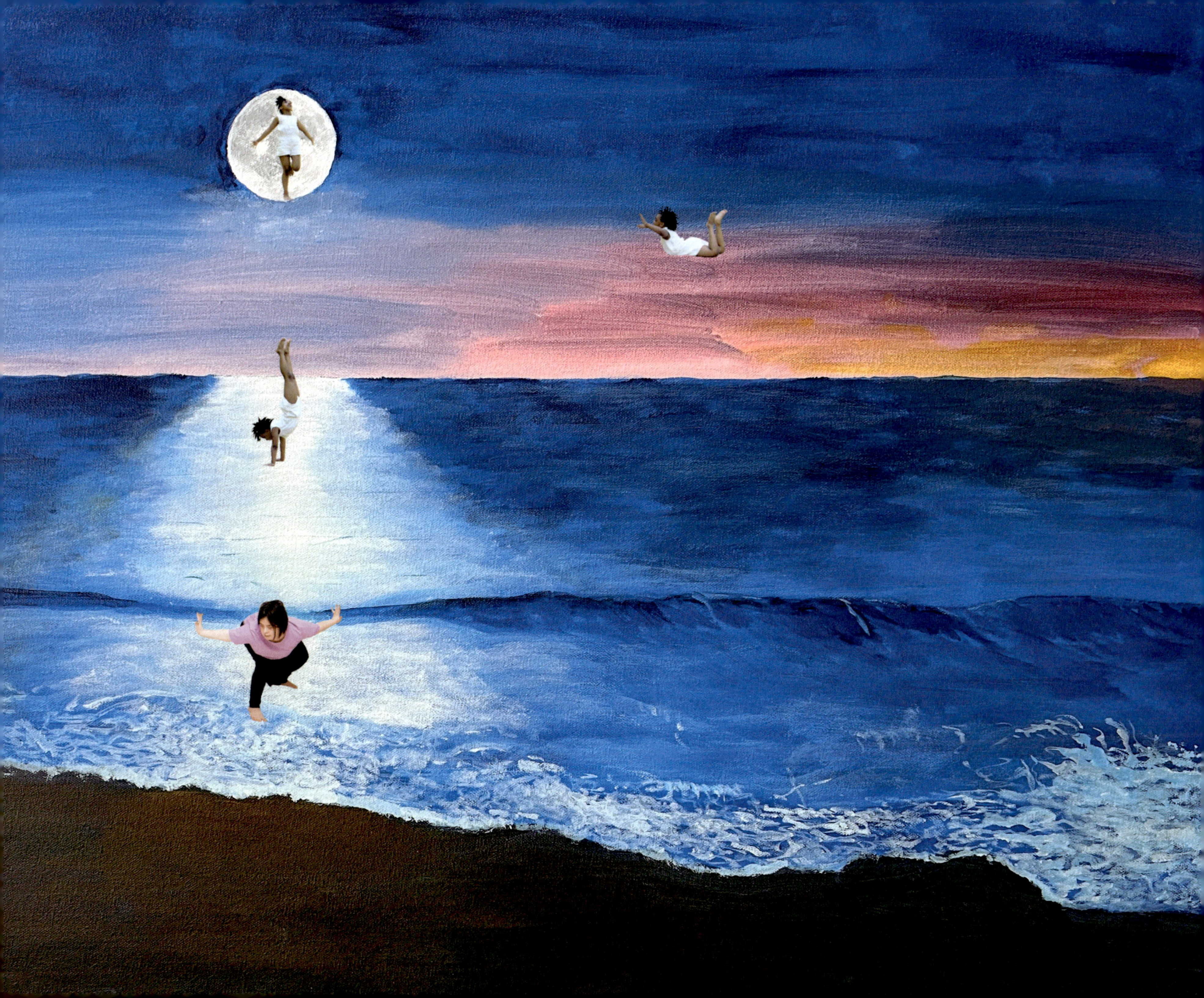

What happens when light travelling in a straight path passes through water or ice?

Refraction

I pass through icicles on a cold and chilly day. Wiggle and bend until all melts away.

Can you find another way to move like bending light?

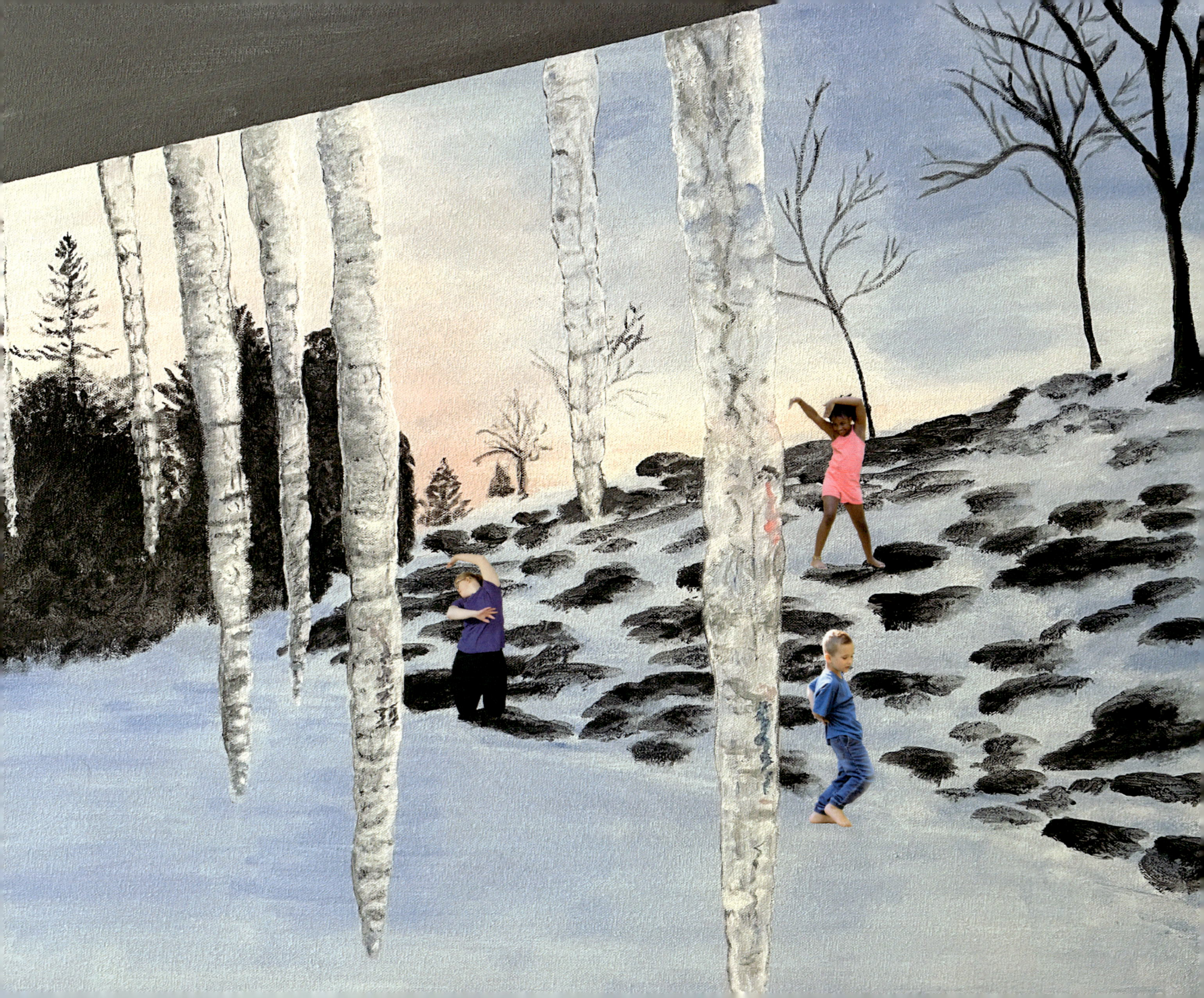

Light from the sun and lamps looks white, but it is really made up of many different colors. What happens when light travels through a prism or raindrop?

Rainbow

I travel from the sun and pass through raindrops in the sky. I arch and curve my colors over the earth from very high.

Can you find another way to move like a rainbow?

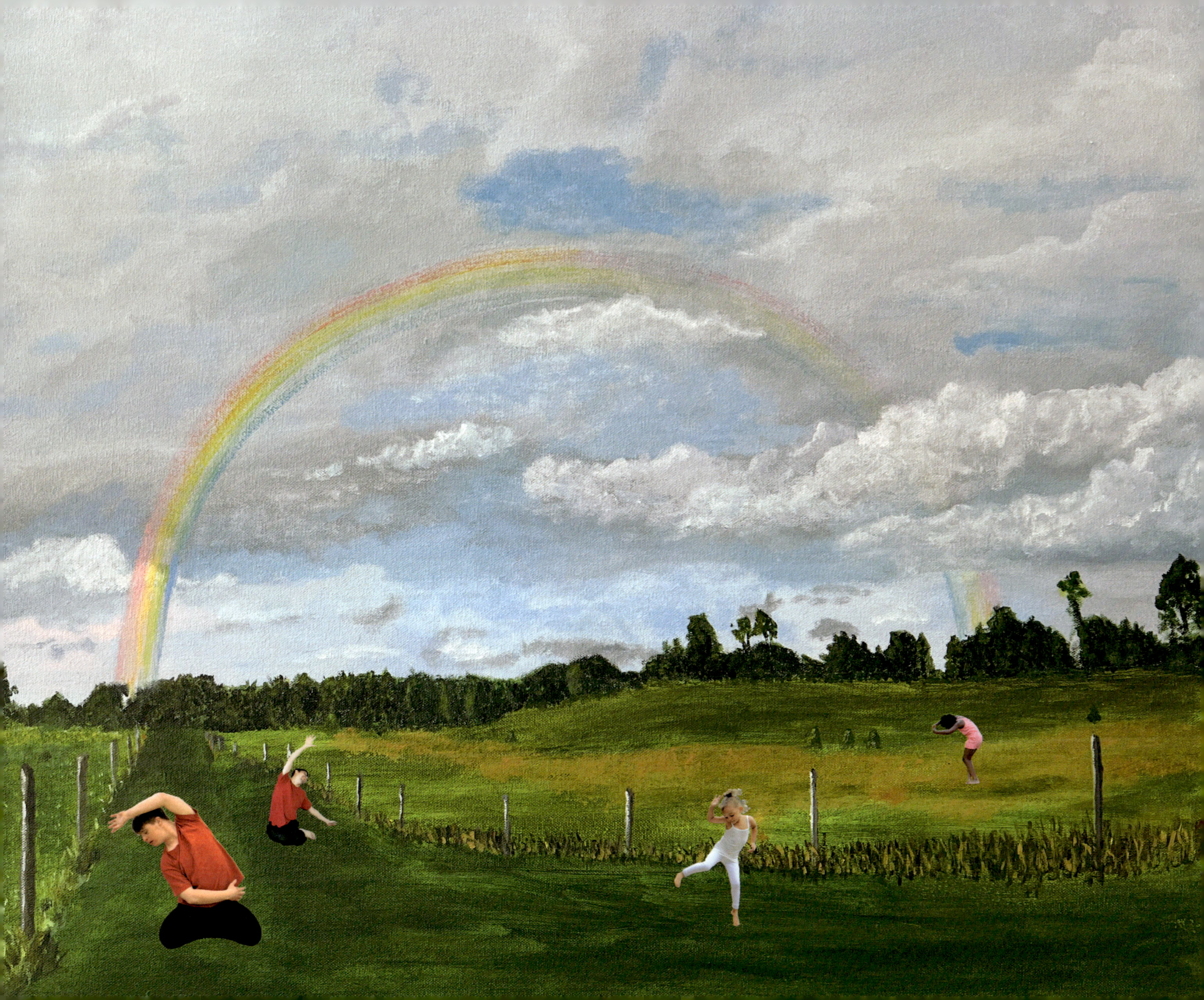

What happens when seeds, soil, air, water, and sunlight combine?

Plants

In the soil, I shoot out, bask, sprout, open, bend and sway.

Can you find another way to move like a growing plant?

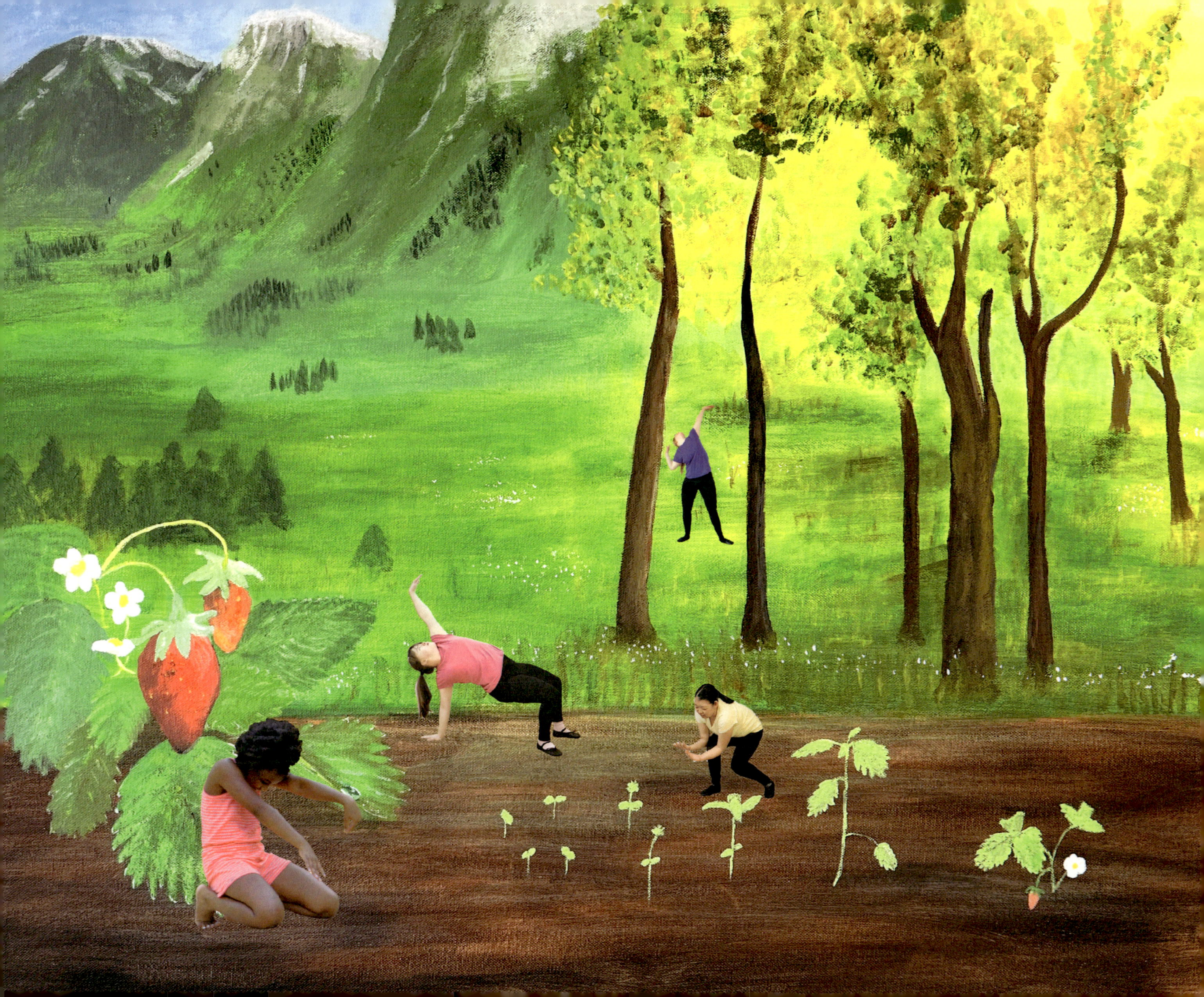

What happens when light is blocked and cannot pass through objects?

Shadows

When light is blocked, I curve, twist, freeze, prance, and wiggle into many shapes.

Can you find another way to make different shadows?

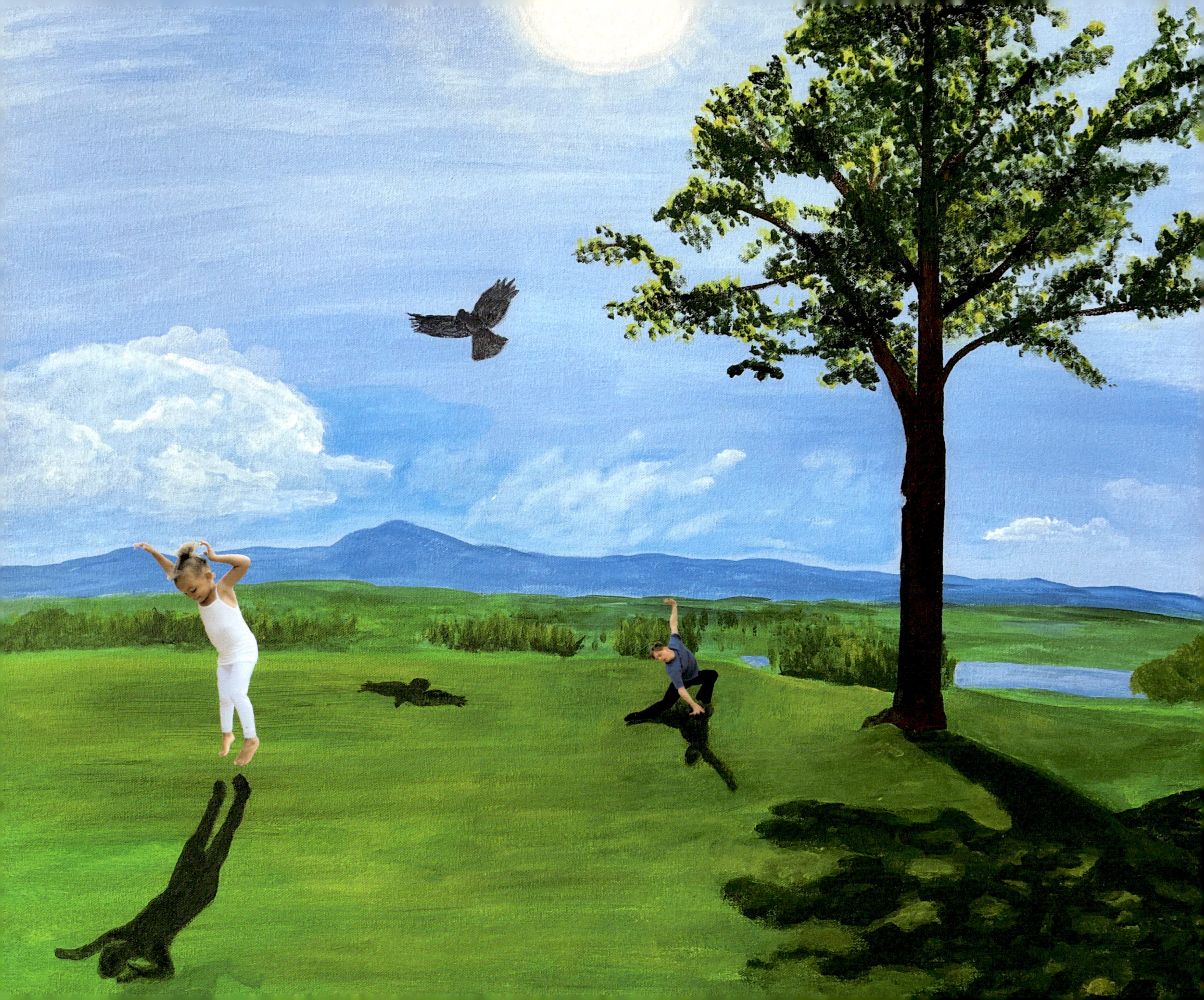

What happens when there is very little light, and it is hard to see?

Darkness

When Earth turns away from the sun's light, it is hard to see. Reach out your arms and make your movements slow. Carefully, carefully you must go!

Can you find another way to move in darkness?

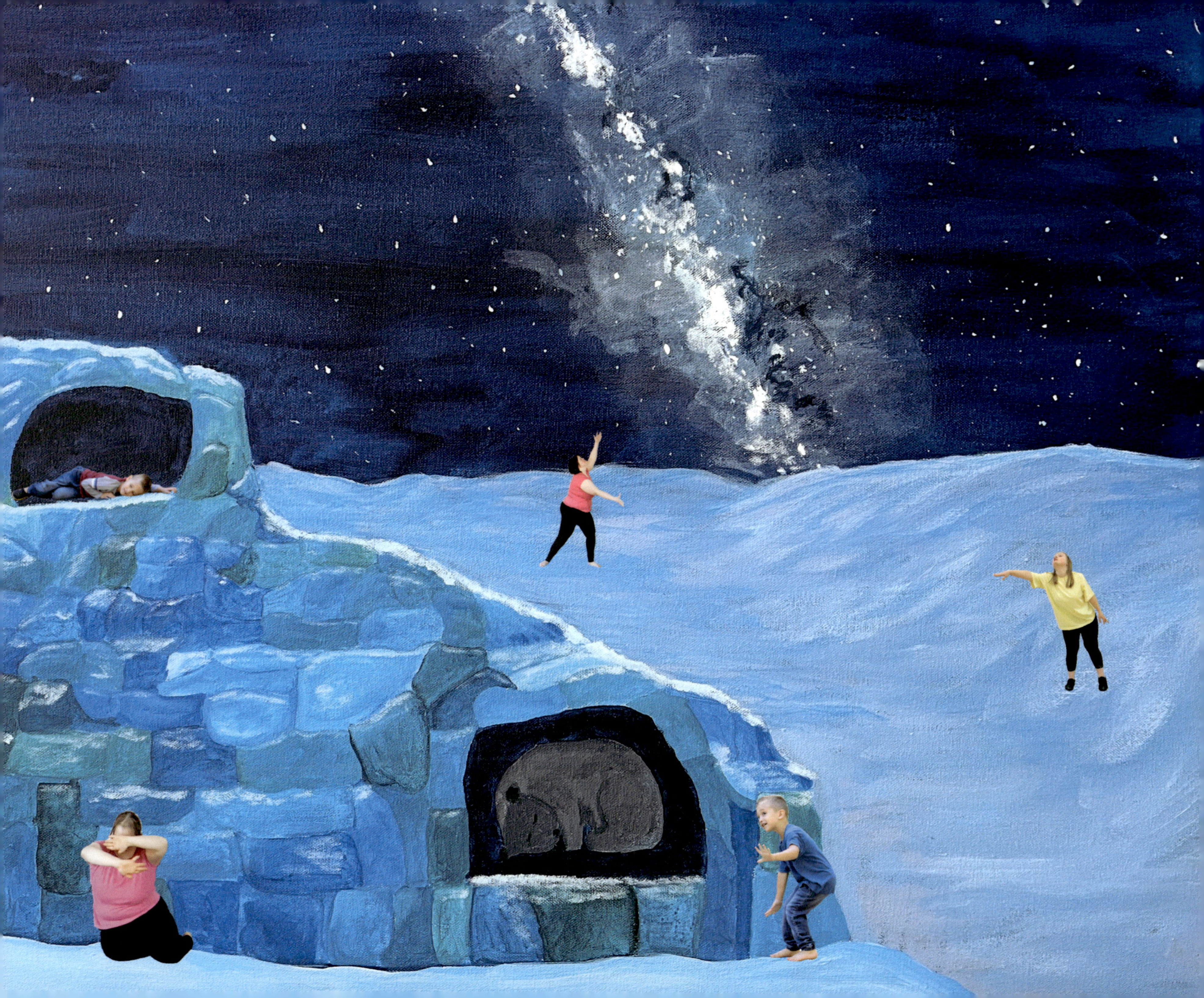

Light comes from many sources and moves in many different ways.

Our Earth

As light, I can make a plant sprout, shine out from a fire, zigzag through a storm cloud, curve like a rainbow, glow and spread from a light bulb, bend inside an icicle, bounce like moonlight, flicker like a firefly, and be blocked to make a shadow or create darkness.

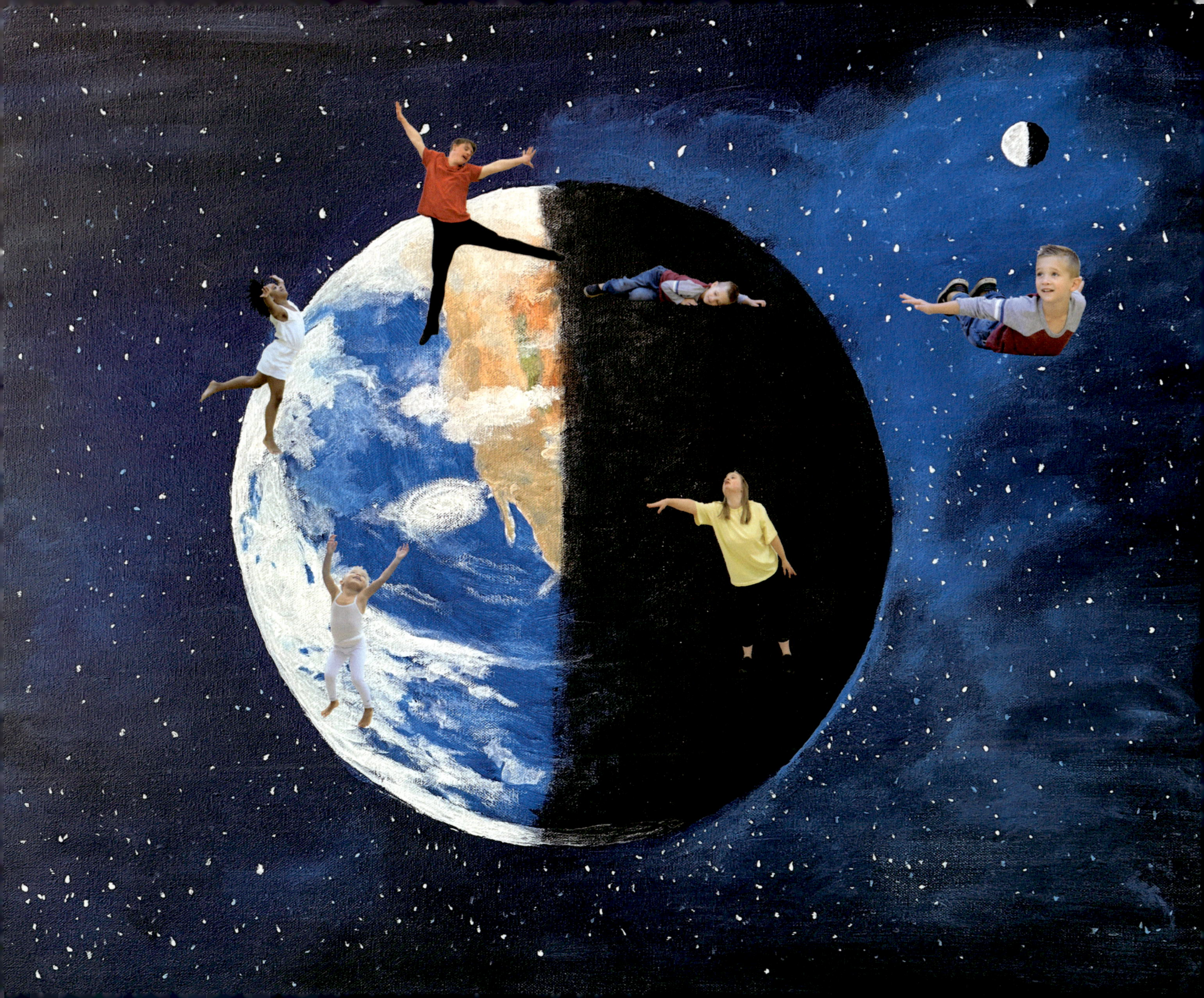

I can make a dance about light.
What will your light dance look like?

Waiting

Block

Look

Bob

Reach

Flicker

Blink

Hover

Brighten

Glow

Launch

Flash

Strike

Bend

Radiate

Swirl Freeze Arch Spread Bud Crisscross

Bask Sprout Expand Sail Sparkle

Grow Prance Open Twist Shine Curve

Bow

Slow

Land

Spark

Fly

Burst

Soar

Lighting

Shaping

Wiggle

Bounce

Pass-through

Rest

Sway

Tips for parents and teachers

Create a dance:

1. Decide on the theme of your dance such as elements in science, stories, art, poetry, music, units of study, etc.
2. Select a variety of action words and different ways to do them that help you illustrate your theme.
3. You can use different body parts, shapes, and qualities such as strength/lightness and quick/slow. You can add different feelings, pathways, directions, and levels. You can be in solos, partners, or groups and use music, words, and props.
4. Create a beginning and an ending.
5. Share your dance with others. Enjoy!

For more ideas go to **www.icanmakeadance.com** and **@icanmakeadance**

YouTube instructional example:
Ocean Dance Lesson **https://youtu.be/iYZrQVQah1Q**

Acknowledgements and Thanks

I would like to acknowledge the wonderful support from my DEL colleagues and associates. Ann Biddle and Deborah Damast have been enthusiastic and supportive of my work for years. Dawn DiPasquale has always been my trusted advisor.

A big thanks to Maryna Bilak Haughton for launching me into the world of visual art making, to Carla Diaz for her editorial eye, and to the photographers Armand Ensanian, Imogen Butler, and Maurice Haughton.

A special thank you to all the wonderful dancers:
Cameron, Elaina, Elise, Irina, and the Tailfeatherdance dancers, Director, Imogen Butler.

Tailfeatherdance provides young adult dancers with learning disabilities a creative platform to explore and develop dance, movement, and performance skills. It believes in promoting inclusivity, celebrating diversity, and widening participation within the performing arts. Thank you, Joshua, Rowan, Catherine, Libby, Sally, Isabel, Kiera, Isabella, Eloise, Blythe, Andrew, Marina, and Eleanor.

Thank you to Lisa Ensanian for her design guidance and layout, and to Armand whose breadth of knowledge in science, language, photography, and publishing was an invaluable resource.

Thank you to my family who have supported me, loved me, and cheered me on!

K.D.E.

About the Author

Karen Diaz Ensanian has devoted her professional life to the dance education of people of all ages. Her extensive experience includes over twenty years as an early childhood educator.

Karen started her early career in New York City as a dancer with several choreographers, including dancing as a founding member with the Alvin Ailey Repertory Company. She later received her M.A. in Dance from The Ohio State University and then taught for nineteen years as Director of Creative Movement at The Episcopal School in The City of New York. Karen also enjoys leading guest workshops at colleges and various organizations. In recent years Karen facilitated Dance Education Laboratory professional development workshops for teachers with the Department of Education in New York City. At the same time, she began teaching herself to paint as a foundation for illustrating a children's dance education book. Karen's debut book *I Can Make a Water Dance* was published in 2021 and has inspired countless young dancers and educators to incorporate dance with the study of natural sciences. *The Dancing Light* is her second book, integrating the art of making dance with the science of light.

Karen currently lives with her husband in NYC where she raised two children.

Lightning Source UK Ltd.
Milton Keynes UK
UKRC031301200422
401789UK00001B/4